EXPLORING

MUMMIES

by
Suzanne Lord

To my Mummy

Published by The Trumpet Club
666 Fifth Avenue, New York, New York 10103

Copyright © 1991 Parachute Press, Inc.

ISBN: 0-440-84423-1

Printed in the United States of America
February 1991

10 9 8 7 6 5 4 3 2 1
CW

PHOTOGRAPH CREDITS

p. 25: top, Neg. No. 254147, Photo B. M. DeCou, Courtesy Department Library Services, American Museum of Natural History; *bottom,* Photography by Egyptian Expedition, The Metropolitan Museum of Art. *p. 26: top,* Bettmann / Hulton; *bottom,* The Bettmann Archive. *p. 27:* The Bettmann Archive. *p. 28:* Courtesy of The Egyptian Museum, Cairo. *p. 29: top,* © Harry Lentz, Art Resource, New York; *bottom,* © Scala, Art Resource, New York. *p. 30:* Neg. No. 335326, Photo A. Singer, Courtesy Department Library Services, American Museum of Natural History. *p. 31: top,* Neg. No. 2A7362, Courtesy Department Library Services, American Museum of Natural History; *bottom,* Photo 14.655. Gift of Robert B. Woodward from the Egypt Exploration Society's excavations of Abydos, 1914. Brooklyn Museum. *p. 32:* The Bettmann Archive.

Cover: The Metropolitan Museum of Art, Rogers Fund, 1912. (12.182.132C)

Contents

Introduction

What Is a Mummy?

British Egyptologist Brian Emery was one of the many people who went to Egypt to study mummies at the turn of the last century. He explored ancient tombs by day. At night he slept in a tent near the tombs. While he slept, the mummy he'd studied that day was placed on a table outside of his tent.

One night Emery jotted down a few last notes about the mummy he was examining. He was ready to go to bed. Then he heard a noise behind him. It sounded like someone coming into his tent. Emery turned to see who it was. What he saw was the withered hand of his mummy opening the tent flap!

1

Emery froze. He was not a superstitious man. But every vein in his body had turned to ice. He was no longer a no-nonsense scientist. For a horrible moment he expected to become a victim of the "mummy's curse"—a superstition he had laughed at before!

The hand stopped. It stayed still. Emery slowly approached the mummy. Only then did he see what had happened. The mummy's table had tilted. As the mummy slid sideways, its hand had caught on Emery's tent flap. It had moved just enough to open the flap—and give Emery a good scare!

Emery shouldn't have worried about a mummy's curse. A mummy can't take revenge if you enter its tomb and unwrap it! A mummy is nothing more than a preserved body. It doesn't matter whether the body is human or animal. It doesn't matter whether the body was preserved on purpose, or whether nature did the job. All preserved bodies are mummies.

Usually when an animal or person dies, its body decays. This decaying process is triggered by oxygen and by the body's own chemicals. When decay is interrupted for a long time, a body becomes preserved. Preservation can occur in one of three ways: by freezing, by chemical means, or by drying.

Some cultures preserved their dead on purpose. Ancient Egyptians and an ancient South American tribe known as the Chinchorros practiced mummification. Both cultures dried the bodies of their dead to preserve them.

Some bodies have been preserved by climatic conditions alone. They are called *natural mummies*. Frozen bodies are an example of natural mummification. Frozen mummies have been found in Alaska, Greenland, and in some cold mountain regions of South America such as northern Chile.

Some natural mummies have been dried, such as Native American mummies in Mesa Verde in Colorado. Nobody "made" them—the bodies were dried by the climate where they were buried.

Other natural mummies have been chemically preserved. These mummies have been found in the peat bogs in the British Isles and in northwestern European countries such as Denmark. The bogs contain acids that preserved the bodies in a process similar to pickling.

Even today some people practice a type of mummification—they have themselves frozen after they die. They believe that in the future, cures may be developed for their ailments. When that day comes, these people hope to be brought back to life. This scientific specialty is called *cryogenics*.

However, the most well-known example of mummies are the ancient Egyptian human mummies. For about 4,000 years (from some time before 3100 B.C. until A.D. 641), Egyptians spent a great deal of time and money preserving the bodies of their dead for eternity. At one time, archaeologists estimate, Egypt had over 500 million mummies!

We have discovered fascinating facts about life in ancient Egypt by studying the remains of people who lived there thousands of years ago.

1

Mummies in Egypt

"Pharaoh is dead!" the priests called out. People ran into the streets of Thebes, weeping. It hardly seemed possible. King Tutankhamen was only eighteen years old.

Throughout Egypt, people went into mourning. They wore special clothes. They stopped bathing. Men stopped shaving. Nobody ate fancy foods or drank any wine. Some people covered themselves with dust.

The pharaoh's dead body was placed in a temporary coffin and taken to the Nile River in a funeral procession. The coffin was rowed across the Nile in a special boat to a *necropolis*—a city of the dead. This is where the pharaoh's corpse would be mummified.

Tutankhamen's body was first washed, oiled, and dressed. Then it was taken to an embalming room, where the body was readied for burial. *Em-*

balmers, people who mummified corpses, began the long process of mummification. A priest read prayers while the body was prepared. The embalming took more than two months. After the embalmers completed their task, the mummified pharaoh got another funeral procession. This one took him to his tomb in the Valley of the Kings, across the Nile from Thebes.

Tutankhamen's tomb was prepared long before he died. Tutankhamen is believed to have been born in 1340 B.C., more than thirty-three centuries ago. The building of his tomb probably began when he became pharaoh at the age of nine in 1331 B.C. The tomb was completed while Tutankhamen's body was being mummified.

The funeral procession stopped at the mouth of the tomb. Priests recited special prayers over Tutankhamen's body and performed rituals such as sacrificing animals. Their purpose was to help Tutankhamen regain all his senses when his mummy entered the tomb. Similar rituals were performed over small statues of humans, called *ushabti.* These prayers would transform the statues into servants for Tutankhamen in his future life.

Finally, the procession entered the tomb. Behind Tutankhamen came hundreds of people. They brought food, furniture, and everything else that a pharaoh might want or need in the afterlife.

When everything was in its proper place, priests said the final prayers. The pathway leading into the burial chamber was sealed. No one would see Tutankhamen until Howard Carter discovered his tomb in 1922.

Tutankhamen's Tomb

It was hot—terribly hot. But that autumn day Howard Carter felt a chill as he gazed at the sealed door in front of him. Carter was the first explorer to discover the mysterious, sealed entrance. He could hardly believe his eyes. The tomb ahead might be the only unlooted royal burial chamber in Egypt. Quickly, he wired to London to have his benefactor and fellow Egyptologist, the wealthy Lord Carnarvon, join him in the Valley of the Kings.

What would they find? Riches? A pharaoh's curse? Or would they face the worst disappointment of all—an empty chamber, looted from another entrance?

Finally the day came when the outer door was opened. Carter shined a flashlight inside the first chamber. Gold was everywhere. The room was stacked with beautiful furniture, chariots, fine plates—everything a king might need or want. The men were overjoyed. It was November 24, 1922, and the world was about to get an early Christmas present—the tomb of young King Tutankhamen, untouched for 3,000 years.

Slowly, they made their way through rooms packed with royal possessions. At last they found a beautiful sarcophagus. Inside, they knew, lay the mummy of the eighteen-year-old pharaoh himself.

Why Did the Egyptians Make Mummies?

In ancient Egypt people worshipped many gods. Some of their gods looked like humans. Some looked like animals. And many had both human and animal features.

Ancient Egyptians believed in life after death. But according to their religion, you needed a preserved body to have an afterlife. They believed that the process of mummification had begun with Osiris and Isis.

Osiris and Isis were said to have lived at the beginning of time. Not only was Osiris a pharaoh and Isis his devoted wife, but they were also a god and goddess with magical powers. They used their powers for the good of their subjects.

But Osiris had an evil brother named Set, who was jealous of him. Set planned to kill Osiris and take over the kingdom. So he had a beautiful box made and dared Osiris to lie down in the box. When Osiris got in, Set's henchmen slammed the lid down, nailed it shut, and threw the box into the Nile. Osiris drowned.

Isis was heartbroken. Not only was her husband dead, but she didn't have his body. She searched and searched until she had recovered Osiris' body. But Set was afraid that Isis would use her powers to bring Osiris back to life. So he grabbed Osiris' body from Isis, sliced it up, and scattered the pieces. Set thought that not even Isis could bring scattered body parts back to life.

Once again, Isis traveled all over Egypt. Eventually she found all fourteen pieces of her husband's body. Isis wrapped the pieces together with linen strips, and Osiris became the first mummy. Then she used her powers to bring Osiris back to life.

The ancient Egyptians believed that they, like Osiris, would have life after death if their bodies were mummified. Even Isis could not have helped Osiris without his preserved, wrapped body. No body, no afterlife!

The First Mummies

Ancient Egyptian history is divided into several periods: Pre-Dynastic (3100–2686 B.C.), Old Kingdom (2575–2130 B.C.), Middle Kingdom (1938–1630 B.C.), New Kingdom (1539–1400 B.C.), and Late Period (664 B.C.–A.D. 639). The years in between are Intermediate Periods of political unrest.

Before 3100 B.C., Egyptians didn't make mummies on purpose. They wrapped their dead in reed mats or baskets. Then they buried the remains in the sand of the nearest desert. Sometimes a body baked under the hot desert sun. When that happened, a natural dried mummy occurred. Scientists believe that the ancient Egyptians started thinking about ways to artificially preserve bodies when they saw naturally preserved ones.

Pharaohs were the first Egyptians to be mummified on purpose. But embalmers were new at their trade and didn't know the best methods for mummification. Over hundreds of years, embalmers experimented with different materials, different wrapping techniques, and different types of burial sites. Some methods worked badly. Others worked well. By trial and error, the Egyptians learned how to make the best mummies.

Old Kingdom mummies were wrapped tightly. Limbs were wrapped separately from the rest of the body. But most Old Kingdom mummies rotted beneath the bandages. The bodies were not sealed well enough against moisture. Today they are nothing more than bags of bones.

Embalmers found better methods of drying bodies during the Middle Kingdom. They used *resin* —a thick, sticky substance obtained from plants —to seal bodies against moisture. They even soaked bandages in resin.

But the very best mummies come from the New Kingdom. This is the period in which King Tutankhamen was mummified. The bodies of some pharaohs were so well preserved that they still look like their carved portraits. We are now able to study the mummies of an entire line of pharaohs. One of them (historians argue over exactly which one) was the pharaoh who had a run-in with Moses!

Late Period mummies were not as well made. Egypt was in a state of great unrest at that time. In earlier times, Egypt had ruled a large empire. During the Late Period, however, Egypt was constantly at war—and losing many of those wars. Little by little, ancient Egypt lost its empire. It was conquered by Persians, then Macedonians, Romans, and Arabs.

During the Late Period, embalmers sometimes didn't have the necessary materials to make a good mummy. And because of the large number of dead warriors, embalmers rushed through the mummification process. When Egypt lost wars, many people felt that their gods had turned against them, and they began to doubt their own religion. This low morale was passed on to embalmers. They felt that their efforts were just pointless old customs that had little to do with religious beliefs. For that reason, many Late Period embalmers did poor work.

Where Were Mummies Buried?

Tombs changed over the years, just as the process of making mummies did. The first tombs were simple pits lined with mud brick to hold back shifting sands. A rectangular structure called a *mastaba* covered each pit. Royalty had bigger mastabas and more underground chambers than did mere nobles.

By 2650 B.C., royal underground pits were covered with triangular structures instead of rectangular ones. These were the first pyramids. One of the first pyramids was the Pyramid of Djoser. This stone structure was built in the necropolis at Saqqara, near modern-day Cairo. It is six stories high, each story smaller than the last. This is called a *step pyramid,* because the layers look like giant steps.

Pyramids grew in size throughout the Old Kingdom (2575–2130 B.C.). The outside no longer looked like steps—the sides of pyramids were now smooth. The underground chambers were more solid and more elaborate. The pyramid itself contained many rooms for the enjoyment of the person who was buried there.

The largest pyramid is the Great Pyramid at Giza. The Pharaoh Khufu (or Cheops) was buried there. It is almost 500 feet tall. Each side of the pyramid measures 252 yards at the base—the length of 2 1/2 football fields! In the Middle Kingdom (1938–1630 B.C.), pyramids became smaller. But pharaohs continued building them.

Members of a pharaoh's family were also buried in chambers within his pyramid. Court nobles, who were not allowed to have pyramids, were buried close to their ruler's pyramid in underground chambers covered with mastabas. Still, their mastabas were very elaborate, sometimes containing an entire temple. Ordinary people were not mummified at all. They continued to be buried in reed mats under the desert sand.

Royalty felt that building great pyramids was proof of their power. Unfortunately, it also showed robbers where the riches lay. By the New Kingdom (1539–1400 B.C.), pharaohs decided to carve tombs in the solid rock of a cliff in a valley near Thebes. Long, horizontal shafts led to burial chambers deep inside the cliff. The entrances to these tombs were hidden.

Ancient Egyptians lived in cities beside the Nile. On the opposite bank of the river, they built necropolises for their dead. Each necropolis had its own government, and was populated by officials, workers, and slaves. These people made a living by making mummies, maintaining tombs, and guarding them against looting. They also received offerings from families of the dead. Some necropolises are Abydos, Saqqara, and Deir al-Bahri (also known as the Valley of the Kings).

At first, a tomb was built for each individual. But this practice proved very expensive. Soon, one tomb was built for each family, with separate chambers for individuals. But people building new chambers for their recently deceased relatives soon began to run into nearby tombs, so families began putting several relatives into one room. By the Late Period, necropolises were seriously overcrowded, so undertakers sometimes put new mummies into old tombs. Scientists occasionally find an Old Kingdom mummy with a much later mummy from the Roman period by its side!

How Were Mummies Made?

The embalmer's first order of business after getting a corpse was to remove the brains. A highly skilled specialist pushed a long, thin, hooklike instrument up through the nose opening until it reached the brain. He then moved the tool back and forth until the brain became mush. With a spoonlike tool he scooped the brain out, bit by bit, through the nose or an eye socket. This process was long and slow. Sometimes an impatient embalmer would lop the head off, pour out the brains through the back of the skull, and bandage the head back on!

Next, another specialist cut a small opening in the body. He removed the intestines, stomach, liver, spleen, and sometimes the kidneys. Then he broke through the diaphragm, reached up inside the body, and cut the windpipe so he could remove the lungs. Since the ancient Egyptians felt that the heart was the center of all feeling, they left it inside the body. If the heart was accidentally cut out, it was wrapped and placed back inside.

Internal organs weren't thrown out—they were washed and dried separately. Then they were wrapped in packets and put into four small containers called *Canopic jars,* which held the intestines, stomach, liver, and lungs. These jars were sealed with wax and usually put back inside the body. In very late mummies, however, Canopic jars were placed between the legs of the mummy.

While the internal organs were being dried and put into jars, the body was placed on a sloping table. The table was covered with dry *natron,* a substance similar to baking powder. Body fluids ran down the slope of the table. A basin placed at one end caught any overflow. Sawdust, chopped straw, and moss stuffing helped dry out the inside of the body. After a little over two months, the corpse was completely dry. The dried body was taken out of its natron "bed," and then washed in perfumed waters or spiced wines and dried with towels. Next, the embalmer coated the body with resin to seal it from moisture.

Now the body was preserved, but it looked like a shriveled prune! So embalmers stuffed the body with anything that would restore its former shape —they used sawdust, cloth, even pottery!

The eyeballs had shrunk, so the embalmers put artificial eyes in the sockets. Some embalmers used small balls of cloth with irises painted on them. One pharaoh had "eyes" of little white onions with painted irises. A princess had white stone eyeballs with black stone irises. Later mummies were given eyes made of wax.

Embalmers made the mummy's shriveled skin look smoother by rubbing perfumed, precious oils all over the body. They made the face look more lifelike by putting cloth pieces up the nose, under the lips, and under the cheeks. Sometimes they even used clay or mud. The body was often painted—red for men and saffron yellow for women. Another coating of resin sealed the body completely from moisture.

Embalmers wrapped the corpse in a *shroud*—a burial garment. Then they brought out the linen bandages. They wrapped fingers and toes separately. Then they wrapped the hands, arms, head, and torso from the top down. Legs and feet were wrapped last. This process was very complicated.

15

It took about two weeks and several pounds of bandages. As the body was being wrapped, the bandages were dipped in resin as another extra seal.

A *funerary mask* was placed over the face and neck of the mummy. Because the mask was supposed to resemble the person, it was molded to the shape of the mummy's face. Tutankhamen's mask of gold is one of the finest in existence. But other masks were made from less expensive materials such as layers of papyrus reeds or cloth. In Roman times, the funerary mask was replaced by a *funerary portrait.* These portraits were painted on flat pieces of wood or sculpted from stucco.

The mummy was then put inside a form-fitting coffin. The coffin was put inside a *sarcophagus,* which is what we now call the *mummy case.* Sometimes mummies were put into three cases— each one fitting inside the next.

Finally, embalmers had to deal with the "leftovers" of embalming. Everything that had come in contact with the body—the natron, the fluid-soaked stuffing, the drying towels—was considered part of the dead person. It had to be packed up and buried with the body. Archaeologists have found jars and sacks full of this waste material. King Tutankhamen's "leftovers" were packed into twelve large jars and placed about 100 yards away from the young pharaoh.

The mummy and its coffin were taken to the necropolis. The coffin was placed in its tomb, which had been made ready with food, drink, and everything else the body would need in its next life.

When an early pharaoh died, his family members and servants were killed and buried with him. He needed these people to serve him in his future life. Then ancient Egyptians figured out a way to stop the killings. They decided that wooden or stone figurines—the *ushabti*—would be able to serve their dead master. Also, paintings and carvings of food and drink were now thought to be as good as the real thing.

This practice enabled people to paint or have statues made of anything they wanted in the afterlife. Almost every aspect of everyday life in ancient Egypt can be found on burial chamber walls. Some people were buried with *ushabti* for every day of the year. The burial chamber walls were covered with pictures of the best food and drink. An elaborately carved miniature boat might be placed in a tomb along with tiny servants to row it. There often were pictures of musicians playing wonderful music for beautiful dancing girls. There could be paintings of hunters and fishermen catching wild game and of people ready for sports or board games!

Animal Mummies

The ancient Egyptians mummified animals as well as humans. Many people wanted their pets to join them in the afterlife. But other ancient Egyptians mummified animals for purely religious reasons. Their gods and goddesses were often symbolized by a particular animal. The popular goddess Bast, for example, was symbolized by a cat. A person who wanted to worship Bast could pay to have a dead cat mummified.

Almost every town in ancient Egypt had certain animals that it treated with special reverence. One town might kick their dogs and mummify their storks. The town next to it might eat their storks and mummify their dogs!

In 1913 archaeologist Camden M. Cobern entered a series of underground tombs in the necropolis of Abydos, downriver from Luxor. In the first tombs he found room after room of stacked jars. Each jar held fifty or more mummies of ibises, a type of Egyptian bird. Some birds were badly wrapped—they fell apart when he touched them. But others were beautifully preserved. Some had been wrapped in lovely multicolored bands. Cobern even found mummified eggs!

A tomb Cobern explored at a later date smelled very bad when he opened it. The tomb consisted of a central passage, 150 feet long and 7 to 10 feet wide, with several side rooms. The entire area was packed with mummified corpses of wild dogs! He had found the Catacomb of Jackals!

Cobern wrote, "There were thousands of skulls of half-mummified heads; bodies broken and mashed; and 2000-year-old bones that crumbled when I touched them."

The ancient Egyptians also mummified sacred bulls, cows, rams, sheep, baboons, falcons, flamingoes, crocodiles, snakes, and some types of fish. They even preserved insects—such as scarab beetles and scorpions!

Who Made Mummies?

Embalmers played an important role in making sure that the dead went on to a proper afterlife. Ancient Egyptians looked upon them with both awe *and* repulsion.

The embalmers worked and lived in the necropolises. A necropolis, like other cities, had a governor who set prices, wrote contracts, and paid everyone from the embalmers right down to the professional mourners and singers. He and his administrators made sure that necropolis workers were well-trained and did good work.

Inside the necropolis, embalmers were treated and paid well. By seeing to the physical embalming, they did the work of the gods. They also performed rituals to guide the person to the afterlife. During these rituals, embalmers sometimes wore a mask representing one of their gods.

Embalmers had slaves assisting them in their work. These assistants washed bodies and internal organs, mixed ointments, and prepared linen bandages.

But embalmers didn't leave their necropolis cities often—they were not respected in the outside world. People who had no hope of being mummified thought of embalmers as men who made a living by putting their hands inside dead bodies. The very idea was repulsive to these common people. Outside of the necropolis, an embalmer had to protect himself and his family from harassment and attacks.

Embalming was a skill that was handed down from father to son. If the sons learned well, necropolis administrators would hire them as full-fledged embalmers.

Not all embalmers were honest and hard-working. Some took advantage of their position. A dishonest embalmer could steal jewelry instead of wrapping it with the body. Or he could substitute a cheap clay ring for the gold one he pocketed.

Mummies After Cleopatra

During the Middle and New Kingdoms, the pharaohs ruled a vast empire. Egypt had been very powerful for thousands of years. Nobody thought that anything could happen to change it. But slowly the empire began to shrink. Rulers and top government officials were assassinated by people who plotted to seize what remained of the country.

Around 47 B.C., Julius Caesar, who controlled the Roman Empire, helped a young Egyptian queen named Cleopatra VII to overthrow her younger brother, Ptolemy XIII. The country still had Egyptian people in high positions, although Cleopatra and Ptolemy were not themselves true Egyptians—they were descendants of Macedonian generals who had conquered Egypt under Alexander the Great almost 300 years before. But after Cleopatra the real rulers became the Romans.

Under Roman rule, Egypt had to pay a vast amount of money each year to Rome. Egypt rapidly became very poor. Only the wealthy citizens received money for cooperating with Rome. Soon they were wearing Roman clothes, fixing their hair in Roman styles, and sometimes even worshipping Roman gods.

Many Egyptians still mummified their dead. But under the Romans it became not so much a religious practice as a tradition. Some people still did it because having relatives mummified showed that a family had money.

In this period, embalmers were paid less. For this reason, and because embalming had no religious meaning anymore, embalmers became sloppy. Instead of carefully sealing each body, they poured "tons" of resin inside and outside bodies. These mummies turned black from too much resin. Today they cannot be unwrapped—they're as hard as cement! Their bandages must be sawed off, the same way a doctor removes a cast. The mummies can't even be X-rayed accurately, because nothing shows up through all the resin.

Lazy embalmers didn't even remove the insides from the body. The four Canopic jars were put in place, but there was nothing in them! Embalmers would also let bodies wait before being mummified. Some bodies lay around for so long that they fell apart during the embalming process. Some mummies are missing fingers, toes, arms, legs, or in some cases—the head! One man had his body cavity stuffed with an arm that had fallen off! And if a mummy was too tall for the available coffin, an embalmer might simply break its legs to make it fit. Or he would lop off the feet.

Appearances were very important to Egyptians in Roman times. People wanted to *look* successful. These mummies were decorated with a lot of jewelry, but it was all imitation. Sarcophagi, or mummy cases, became lavish works of art, while the bodies inside were carelessly preserved.

Funerary portraits came into fashion after the Romans conquered Egypt. There are two types of funerary portraits. One type is known as *Antinöe portraits*. They are three-dimensional sculptures of a person's head made from stucco. They show the head leaning forward, supported on a small pillow. Antinöe portraits were fitted onto the top part of the sarcophagus lid.

The other type of funerary portraits is called *Faiyum portraits*. They are found on many mummies from the Faiyum area in northern Egypt. These beautiful, lifelike depictions were painted on flat wooden boards. People had their pictures painted when they were young, and had expensive jewels painted on their portraits, whether they owned any or not. The boards were placed over the mummy's face, and held in place by the mummy's bandages. Hundreds of these painted images have been discovered and are often shown in museums or art galleries. The edges of the portraits fade out because they were supposed to be covered by mummy bandages.

It was during this time that the necropolises really became overcrowded. Instead of having private rooms, mummies were stacked up like pieces of wood. Many families no longer had space to put relatives in the family tomb. Undertakers became wealthy in bidding wars for available necropolis chamber space.

Because of the crowding, coffins were made smaller. Some were mass-produced—they were sold completely finished except for the face. Cheap coffins were hardly decorated at all. The corpse inside had only an identification tag with its name, date of birth, and date of death on it. A thriving trade in secondhand coffins started up. Looters would dump the original body, take the name off, and resell the coffin.

Romanized Egyptians began keeping mummies of relatives in their houses, perhaps because of necropolis overcrowding. But some families may have wanted to show off their fancy mummy cases, since most people could no longer afford them. Some of these cases didn't even have mummies in them. They were bought well before a person died. Living people would have their coffins made early, and keep them in the house for later use. Many times coffins were damaged by water dripping in through roof leaks. Others were used as shelves. We know this because these coffins are covered with olive oil and other liquid spills!

Mummification Dies Out

Gradually, mummification had become an expensive and outdated custom. Christianity became the important religion in Egypt as many people adopted Christian beliefs. According to Christians, only a person's spirit, or soul, is eternal—a dead body is something to be left behind, not preserved, when a person dies. When Moslems invaded Egypt in A.D. 639, they felt the same way. The Moslem conquerors even made new laws forbidding mummification. After almost 4,000 years, the Egyptian practice of making mummies died out.

King Tutankhamen's tomb lies in the Valley of the Kings, below the entrance to the tomb of Rameses VI.

The burial chamber of King Tutankhamen was the greatest discovery of Howard Carter's career.

King Tutankhamen's coffin is the only gold mummiform coffin in the world.

The pharaoh Rameses II lived from about 1292 to 1225 B.C. Each finger of his mummy is wrapped individually.

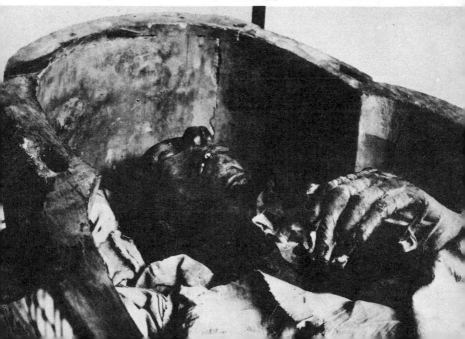

This ancient Egyptian mummy is so well preserved that we can tell what the man looked like when he was alive.

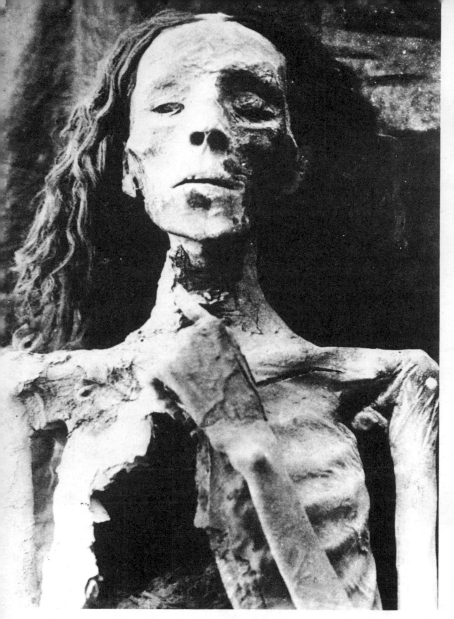

No one knows the exact identity of this royal woman, found in the tomb of the ancient Egyptian pharaoh Amenhotep II.

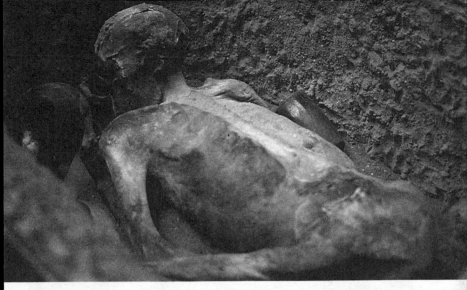

This mummy in an open sarcophagus from about 3300 B.C. was found in Upper Egypt.

The mummy of King Tutankhamen, encased in three coffins, lay within this sarcophagus.

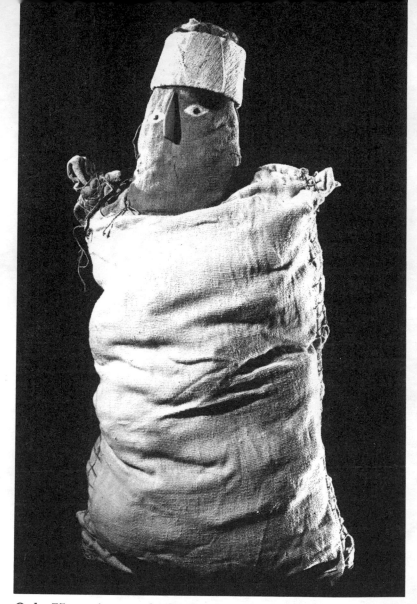

Only 75 centimeters high, this Peruvian mummy pouch was made to hold a small child. It has a cloth head, painted eyes, and a wooden nose.

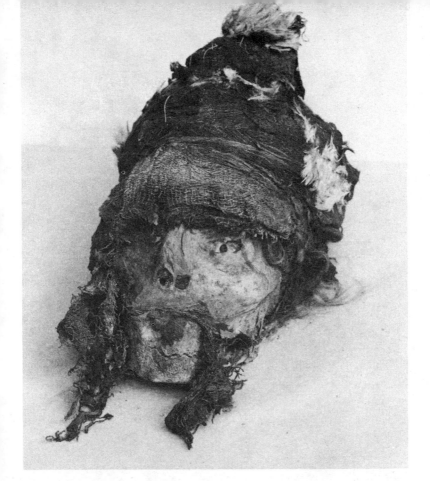

This partially unwrapped head of a mummy was found near Paracas, Peru.

Ancient Egyptians mummified animals to honor their gods. This is a preserved ibis.

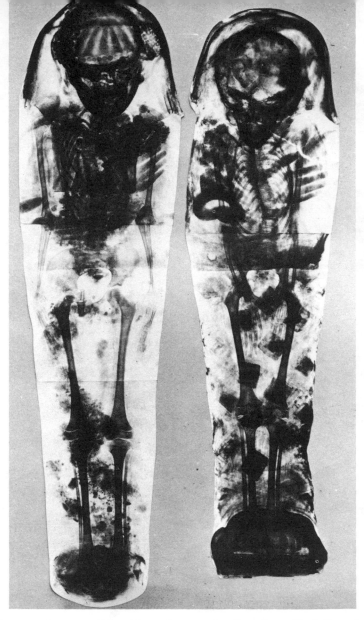

X rays of two ancient Egyptian mummies show that they had curved spines, a common ailment even today. They are a sister *(left)* and brother *(right)*.

2

Mummies for Fun, Profit, and Chills

At the time the Moslems conquered Egypt in A.D. 639, most of the country was Christian. After that, many people became Moslems. Nobody worshipped the ancient Egyptian gods anymore.

Trade brought Europeans to Egypt after A.D. 1000. Europeans also came to the Middle East from 1059 to 1291 to fight the religious wars between Moslems and Christians called the Crusades. They brought tales of Egyptian mummies back home, and soon mummies became an object of fascination in Europe.

Europeans began to believe that mummies must have something to do with living a long time because they had been preserved for so many years.

Mummies as Medicine

As early as 1100, both Arab and Christian doctors began prescribing a medicine called "mummy" for their patients. At first, "mummy" meant the resin used to seal mummies' body cavities. "Mummy" was used as a cheaper, more available substitute for asphalt, a kind of mineral pitch that was another popular medicine of the time. In 1203 an Arab doctor wrote that "mummy" was "sold for a trifle. I purchased three heads filled with the substance."

Sometimes substances other than resin were sold as "mummy." An Arab reported in the 1400's that some Cairo citizens had been arrested for removing corpses from tombs and boiling them in water. Then they collected the oil that rose to the surface of the liquid in order to sell it to the French.

At some point, "mummy" stopped meaning resin and started meaning ground-up dead people! Flesh from the mummy itself was ground into a powder and sold as medicine. This could be made into a cream to rub onto bruises and wounds, or it could even be mixed into food or tea to be taken internally! In the 1600's, a person in Scotland could buy a pound of "mummy" for only 8 shillings.

"Mummy" was supposed to stop bleeding. Many medieval doctors also prescribed it for a variety of ailments such as fractures, paralysis, migraine, epilepsy, coughs, nausea, disorders of the liver and spleen, and cases of poisoning.

In those days, the Egyptians were only too happy to sell the mummies. People no longer thought of them as relatives. Mummies not only cluttered up the country, but they were easy to find. And people needed the money. Tomb robbers were very busy during this period, though stealing mummies was against the law.

Trade in "mummy" was a thriving business for 400 years. French kings and Italian nobles kept a supply of it in their homes—just as we keep aspirin around in case of a headache.

As the supply of mummies began to run out, a horrible practice sprang up. Corpses of beggars, criminals, and people who had died of diseases were dried, made into "instant mummies," and sold as the real thing.

European doctors eventually began to doubt that mummies were actually medicinal. Ambrose Paré, a French surgeon who practiced in the 1600's, wrote in his medical journal about the use of "mummy." He felt it was disgusting that people thought ancient Egyptians had been carefully preserved just so they "might serve as food and drink for the living." He wrote that "not only does this wretched drug do no good to the sick . . . but it causes them great pain in their stomachs, gives them evil-smelling breath, and brings on serious vomiting which is more likely to stir up the blood and worsen hemorrhaging than to stop it." Paré ended by saying that the only good use for "mummy" was as fishing bait!

Mummies for Money

In the 1800's, traders who called themselves "scientific collectors" gathered up shiploads of Egyptian mummies and other objects found in burial chambers. They sold their wares as "antiquities" to the highest bidder. Museums, private collectors, and even carnivals wanted mummies. And the poor Arab Egyptians were only too happy to sell them.

In the early 1800's, mummy unwrapping became a popular social event. Everyone wanted to see a mummy. People would pay money to get as close as possible to them and to watch them being unwrapped. Mummies were even unwrapped in some homes to entertain guests. Sometimes the host would serve supper during an unwrapping!

Once 600 people showed up in London to watch surgeon Thomas J. Pettigrew perform a mummy autopsy. Unfortunately, the mummy was one of the later, resin-soaked kind. He couldn't unwrap it. He couldn't pry it open, and hammers and chisels did no good either. After three hours, Pettigrew gave up, leaving his patrons *very* disappointed.

Strange Uses for Mummies

Egyptians thought their supply of mummies

was endless. They ground up mummies in order to fertilize local crops. Sometimes they used mummies instead of thatch to roof their houses. They even chopped up wooden mummy cases to use as firewood for cooking. Some Italians paneled their homes with coffin wood!

One of the strangest uses for mummies came about in Canada and America. During the 1860's, paper manufacturers in both countries bought shiploads of mummies. They used the mummies' linen wrappings to make wrapping paper!

In the nineteenth century, when Egyptians built trains as a new means of transportation, the Egyptian railroads bought mummies to burn as a cheap source of fuel. Mummies were not only filled inside and out with resin, they were also as dry as tinder. No wonder they burned so well!

Egyptology

Why were so many Europeans and Americans going to Egypt in the nineteenth century? Why was there worldwide interest in learning more about ancient Egyptian culture?

For centuries no one had understood Egyptian history. Of course, people had seen mummies, huge statues, and crumbling ruins of ancient cities and temples. People had examined whatever remained of ancient Egypt. Yet they actually knew little about it, because no one was able to read Egyptian writing, called *hieroglyphics*.

Then, during Napoleon's Egyptian campaign in

1799, the famous Rosetta Stone was discovered. On this stone, the same message had been carved in three languages. One was ancient Egyptian hieroglyphics; another was a different Egyptian dialect; the third was ancient Greek. By 1821 a language specialist named Jean-François Champollion had used the Greek, which he understood, to figure out what the hieroglyphics meant. A whole new and mysterious world opened up, and Champollion became known as the father of what was called Egyptology.

The Western world soon became fascinated with Egyptology. In the late 1800's and early 1900's, teams of scientists from many countries combed Egypt for artifacts. They wanted to know who the ancient Egyptians were—how they lived, what diseases they had, who they worshipped, and what their world was like.

During the early days of Egyptology, collectors were one of two types. The first type was a sincere scientific collector. The second type was interested only in making money. One of the best antiquities collectors of all time was of the second type. His name was Giovanni Battista Belzoni.

Belzoni was an adventurer. At 6½ feet tall, he had once been a carnival strongman. He loved to travel and see new places and people. Belzoni originally came to Egypt in 1815 to build a waterwheel for a local ruler. But soon he realized what huge profits he could make in "antiquities."

Belzoni bribed and bullied his way into tombs. He came away with huge collections of mummies, papyrus rolls, and artifacts. Belzoni wasn't picky about what he took or where he got it. He looted royal tombs as well as mummy-stuffed underground caverns. Of course, all this was illegal, but Belzoni's only goal was to collect as many artifacts as he could. Then he planned to get out alive and sell them all!

At first, Belzoni didn't think he could "put my face in contact with that of some decayed Egyptian" while squeezing his huge frame through narrow passages. But soon he got used to his line of work. He declared, "I would have slept in a mummy pit as readily as out of it."

Even so, he admitted it was a bizarre job. "Surrounded by bodies, by heaps of mummies in all directions . . . the blackness of the wall, the faint light given by the candles or torches for want of air, the different objects that surrounded me, seeming to converse with each other, and the Arabs with the candles or torches in their hands, naked and covered with dust, themselves resembling living mummies, absolutely formed a scene that cannot be described."

After four years, Belzoni was driven out of Egypt. When a rival collector named Drovetti almost killed him, Belzoni realized that his life really was in danger! He left Egypt with the last of his loot and never returned. Today most people are disgusted by Belzoni's Egyptian exploits, but the British Museum cannot complain. Their Egyptian Hall is stuffed to the rafters with Belzoni's pirated treasure!

Egyptologists were not all like Belzoni. Many were honest scientists, or dedicated amateurs. They explored pyramids and necropolises, making careful notes of their finds. They treated all the artifacts as remnants of a proud culture. Serious Egyptologists saved many mummies from destruction by reckless looters.

But thieves often beat the Egyptologists to their goal of an untouched (preferably royal) tomb. Some tombs were found intact. But until 1922 no one had ever found an untouched royal tomb.

The discovery of Tutankhamen's tomb was incredibly exciting. It was the only royal tomb looters had never plundered. Everything was exactly the way it had been left on the day King Tutankhamen was buried. This is one reason why this pharaoh continues to fascinate people today.

The Mummy's Curse

Part of the "mummy's curse" legend is true. Usually rumors are based at least partly on truth —and nearly all mummies were buried with printed curses, booby traps, and false trails to discourage thieves. But millions of mummies were violated anyway. Not even the pharaohs escaped the greed of looters.

And yet sometimes the mummy's curse seemed to work! In 1905 an Egyptian family began to disappear, one by one. The father had discovered a corridor leading to a burial chamber. Hoping to find treasure there, he found instead that the air had become poisonous over the years. Each time one person went to find the others, he passed out and died. When the police investigated the disappearances, they almost died, too! The health department told people that bad air killed the family. But many chose to believe that mummies protecting their riches had strangled the unwelcome visitors.

Rumor had it that anyone who had taken part in the opening of King Tutankhamen's tomb was cursed. It started with the death of Lord Carnarvon, the wealthy British Egyptologist who had funded Howard Carter's search for Tutankhamen's tomb. When Carter found the sealed tomb entrance, he notified Carnarvon immediately. Carnarvon and several reporters came for the official opening on November 24, 1922. Carnarvon was already sick, but a mosquito bite caused him to become very ill soon after the tomb opening. By early April he was dead. Six months later, Lord Carnarvon's half-brother died. So did the nurse who had tended Lord Carnarvon in his illness. A doctor named Archibald Douglas Reed died in 1924 soon after X-raying Tutankhamen's mummy. In addition, an American, an English businessman, and a Canadian tourist all died within 24 hours of viewing the tomb. The list goes on and includes museum antiquities keepers, Lord Carnarvon's wife, Howard Carter's secretary, the secretary's father (who committed suicide from grief), and even a little boy run over by the secretary's father's hearse!

No one paid much attention to those people who survived. Howard Carter lived a full life, and the man who actually unwrapped Tutankhamen lived to be eighty years old. Still, Lord Carnarvon's death and the string of deaths that followed made the "mummy's curse" a worldwide superstition.

3

Mummies Around the World

One society besides ancient Egypt practiced mummification—the Chinchorros, an ancient South American Indian society. At least one of the Chinchorro mummies has been dated at 7,800 years old! In contrast, the oldest Egyptian mummies are only 4,000 years old.

Chile and Peru

The Chinchorros lived near the Pacific Ocean, close to the border between Chile and Peru. They fished with nets and hunted sea lions and seabirds. But we have no written records or pictures of their lives. Their mummies and the artifacts they were buried with are all we have left of their culture. So scientists are still not sure just why the Chinchorros made mummies. Some believe

43

that the Chinchorros mummified only outstanding tribe members and their families.

However, scientists do know one thing for sure —they know how Chinchorro mummy-makers did their work. Chinchorro embalmers first removed the internal organs through an incision in the body's chest. They also removed the brain, hair, and some major muscles. They dried the inside of the body with hot coals and ashes. After filling the hollow body with feather-and-wool stuffing, they inserted sharp wooden rods from the ankles to the base of the skull to keep the body stiffly upright. Next they sealed the entire body with an airtight clay covering. Then they put the hair back on over the clay and painted the clay. Finally they buried the mummy standing up.

Chinchorro mummies were buried close to the Pacific Ocean in what is now the city of Arica, in Chile. But the clay there stays dry. Atmospheric conditions in the area cause ocean winds to lose their moisture, so it almost never rains in Arica. And when rains do come, they are not heavy enough to sink deeply into the soil.

Egyptian mummies are now rare. But citizens of Arica can hardly plant a garden without uprooting a mummy! To Aricans, the mummies are a source of income. Tourists have been offered the feet, heads, and hands of mummies for prices of ten dollars and up. Other Arican citizens see the mummies as a big nuisance. "Every time we dug in the garden or dug to add a section to our house, we found bodies," one woman complained. "Then

I started to get used to it. We'd throw their bones out on the hill and the dogs would take them away."

Scientists are worried about losing the remaining Chinchorro mummies—the oldest man-made mummies in the world. They want to study Chinchorro remains in order to learn about the history of certain diseases. For example, tuberculosis was always believed to have been brought to America by the Europeans. But now we know that some Chinchorros had the disease thousands of years before Europeans arrived.

Scientists have also learned a lot about Chinchorro life from the mummies. Many women have healed-over fractures on their faces and arms. They might have been beaten at home. Many men show deafness from ear infections. These infections probably resulted from years of ocean diving.

Scientists are racing to study Chinchorro mummies before they are all destroyed. But even as they work, they hear mothers scolding their children, "Don't play with those bones—mummies give you pimples!"

A Sleeping Inca

In recent years, an eight- or nine-year-old boy, naturally mummified by freezing, was discovered on the El Plomo peak in Chile at an altitude of 17,712 feet. Scientists believe that some 500 years ago Incan priests had chosen him to be a sacrifice

45

to the sun goddess. The boy wore fine stitched slippers and a beautiful blanket. His hair was plaited into hundreds of tiny braids, and he also wore a feather-and-gold headdress.

When the priests reached the top of the mountain, the boy was probably told to wait for the goddess inside a cave. Beside him were found a llama doll and a doll that looked like the sun goddess.

The priests closed the cave's entrance. The boy wrapped himself in his blanket. It was very, very cold. He chewed on a coca leaf and probably fell asleep before he froze to death.

The boy remained sealed in the cave for five centuries before archaeologists found him. His corpse was so well preserved that he looked as though he might wake up any minute. His frozen body is now on display in a deep-freeze showcase in a museum in Santiago, Chile.

European Mummies

Ancient Europeans and ancient Egyptians had very different beliefs about death and the afterlife. The Egyptians believed that a preserved body was necessary for the dead person's spirit to have a proper afterlife. The Europeans, in contrast, believed that the spirit of a dead person left the aches, pains, and troubles of the body *behind* for the afterlife. For this reason, Europeans did not mummify the remains of their dead on purpose.

However, there have been cases of natural

mummification in the British Isles and elsewhere in Europe. Peat bogs in Denmark have preserved several bodies remarkably well. Nobody knows why certain people were buried in peat-moss bogs. Perhaps they were criminals who were executed, or perhaps they were sacrificed to an ancient god.

A peat bog is a large swamplike area filled with moss and water. Peat contains a lot of acid, which seeps into the water. The acidic water stops oxygen and bacteria from decomposing bodies buried in the bogs. People have been discovering mummies in peat bogs since the 1700's. But so far, the most remarkable mummy discovered has been Denmark's Tollund man.

In 1950 peat cutters (people who gather peat from bogs for use as fuel and fertilizer) discovered the body of a man in a bog. They thought he was someone who had been killed the week before!

The peat cutters called the police. But the policeman pointed out that the man *couldn't* have died recently—the body was found under 7 feet of peat!

The policeman called in P. V. Glob, a professor at Denmark's Aarhus University. Professor Glob had the body dug out from the peat.

"As dusk fell," he wrote, "we saw in the fading light a man take shape before us. He was curled up . . . as if asleep. His eyes were peacefully shut. . . . That his rest had lasted 2,000 years was clearly shown by the seven feet of peat which had gradually formed above him throughout the centuries."

The man was naked except for a cap, a belt—
and a noose around his neck! But scientists con-
cluded that Tollund man was *not* a criminal—he
had been sacrificed to the gods his people worshipped.

Tollund man's skin was dyed a deep brown by
the acidic peat. Otherwise, he looked very much
as he did 2,000 years ago!

Colorado's Mummy Cave

Mesa Verde National Park in Colorado contains
some of the finest prehistoric Native American
dwellings in America. These dwellings were
carved into the side of a cliff at least seventeen
centuries ago. All the dwellings are high above
the surrounding land, where they were easy to
defend against animal and human enemies. The
cliff also provided protection from bad weather.

We do not know the name of the people who
once lived in the Mesa Verde cliff dwellings. But
both Navajo and Hopi tribes believe that these
ancient people were their ancestors. Both tribes
call the ancient cliff dwellers *Anasazi,* which
means "ancient ones."

The Anasazi did not bury their dead below their
cliff dwellings. They may have worried that wild
animals or enemies would disturb the bodies. Instead, they buried them in deep caves *behind*
their living quarters. Because of the exceptional
dryness of the region, these bodies became natural mummies.

Mexican Mummies

In the Mexican city of Guanajuato there is a large collection of natural mummies that has grown over several centuries. Bodies are first placed in aboveground crypts. They are not embalmed—they simply dry out and are eventually moved to an underground crypt when the aboveground one becomes too crowded. Propped up in rows, they appear very lifclike. Even today, bodies are added to the mummy collection at Guanajuato.

Mummies in Greenland and Alaska

Ancient peoples who lived in Alaska and Greenland sometimes piled several people into wood-lined burial houses or into underground pits. In the 1790's, travelers found bodies in the Aleutian Islands that had been embalmed—stuffed with moss and hay after the internal organs had been removed. Sometimes these bodies had frozen and remained frozen, becoming natural mummies.

In the late 1920's, Harold McCracken, a big-game hunter in Alaska, heard stories about frozen mummies called *asxi'nan,* or departed ones. One Eskimo told McCracken that he knew about a grave site on Fortress Island, one of the Aleutians. McCracken dug at the site and discovered four frozen mummies—two men, a woman, and a baby.

"I touched it," he wrote. "The hand of a Stone Age human mummy of the Arctic!"

Years later, in 1977, a team of scientists from Denmark and Greenland uncovered a 500-year-old Inuit burial site in Greenland. They found two grave sites with a total of eight bodies in them. At first they thought they had found seven bodies and a doll, but the "doll" proved to be a six-month-old baby! All of these mummies are now on display in the museum at Nuuk, in Greenland.

4

Secrets of the Mummies

In 1881 twenty-seven royal mummies were discovered in Deir-al-Bahri—the Valley of the Kings. These mummies had been looted by tomb robbers in about 1100 B.C. An ancient Egyptian family had actually hidden the mummies themselves for generations, to keep them safe. The Egyptian government decided that the royal mummies would be safest in a museum in Cairo.

The pharaohs were carefully taken outside for the first time in thousands of years. The mummies were loaded onto a boat that took them back down the Nile, past where they had once lived and ruled the Egyptian empire. According to the laws at that time, Cairo officials had to assess everything coming into the city for tax purposes. But what was a mummy? Cloth? Meat? An antique? The twenty-seven priceless pharaohs finally entered the city—assessed as dried fish!

Techniques of Studying Mummies

Studying a mummy used to mean unwrapping it and looking inside. But today mummies are rarely opened. When they are, they are handled very carefully.

Scientists, doctors, dentists, disease specialists, a photographer, and many other professionals are usually present. And the entire procedure is videotaped.

First, the mummy is X-rayed. The X ray shows how the body is laid out and whether any jewelry or charms were wrapped with the body. Then the mummy gets a *CAT scan*. Usually these scans are used on living people to locate tumors inside the body. On mummies, they indicate where skin ends and bandages begin. Computer graphics can even translate the scan into a picture of the ancient Egyptian!

Next comes the difficult task of removing the bandages. There may be anywhere from ten to twenty layers of linen strips. These strips were all soaked in resin, and the outer layer was also sealed with resin. Over thousands of years, resin turns into a substance as hard as cement! Bandages often must be removed with a hammer and chisel, and sometimes a saw has to be used. It took nine people 7 hours to remove one mummy's bandages! While this work is going on, other specialists remove the mummy's organs from its four Canopic jars if they are found outside the body cavity.

When the mummy is exposed, its skin is like plastic. A newly unwrapped mummy may have light brown skin. But within 24 hours, it turns brownish black. Before that point, scientists might use an *endoscope,* an instrument consisting of a miniature camera and light attached to a thin wire. It is put inside the mummy through a small incision. It enables scientists to see what the mummy looks like inside before they unwrap it.

As the mummy is opened, specialists study the parts they are interested in. A cardiologist may look at the heart while a dentist examines the teeth. Pathologists look for diseased tissue. Bone specialists look for spinal defects, healed-over fractures, or signs of arthritis.

Rehydration is one way to study a mummy's organs. Mummies are much like dried mushrooms—mummy parts placed in water swell back into their original shape. Scientists can "revive" organs, blood cells, and even shrunken eyeballs. Using both regular and electron microscopes, they can study these organs closely. Scientists can tell a mummy's blood type, whether or not its arteries are clogged, and the condition of the lungs.

Sometimes a scientist will try something really unusual. Svante Paabo, a Swedish biologist, recently tried to clone DNA (genetic material found in living cells) from a 2,400-year-old mummy! The cloning didn't work because the DNA strands were incomplete. Paabo later said that even with complete strands, the material would have been too jumbled to reconstruct.

What Mummies Tell Us

Scientists have learned from mummies that in ancient Egypt the average life expectancy was 51.6 years for a man and 53.8 years for a woman.

The ancient Egyptians had terrible teeth. There was so much grit in their bread that it slowly but surely wore down their teeth. The grit came from the fields where the grain was grown, from metal and wood fragments of threshing tools, from sand picked up during winnowing—or separating—the grain from the straw, from more sand blowing into grain-storage areas, from bits of mortar and pestle used to grind the grain into flour, *and* from minerals added to make the flour finer.

Dental work found on mummies was done *after* the person was dead, before the body was mummified!

Many Egyptians' lungs look like those of cigarette smokers. Cooking fires in poorly ventilated rooms and a life of inhaling sand crystals clogged their lungs.

We can tell from their mummies that royalty had their share of disease and other physical problems. Pharaoh Pum II suffered from hardening of the arteries. Princess Makare died in childbirth. The Pharaoh Siptah had a shortened leg from polio. The Pharaoh Merenptah may look thin now, but he was fat when he was alive. Ta-Bes, a noblewoman, had a curved spine.

5

Mummies Today

In 1977 the Egyptian Museum in Cairo discovered a *real* mummy's curse: Pharaoh Rameses II, one of the museum's finest mummies, was covered with sixty types of fungi and two kinds of insects! Horrified officials rushed the pharaoh's valuable mummy to Paris in a special sealed crate in order to clean it up.

The Egyptian Museum houses twenty-seven royal mummies. Examinations proved that the other twenty-six royal mummies weren't in very good shape either! The President at the time, Anwar Sadat, removed all the mummies from public view. Since then, scientists all over the world have argued about how to preserve the mummies. Meanwhile, they are the only people who get to see most of them.

Preserving the Preserved

Ancient Egyptian mummies are now rare. The ones we have must be preserved so that future generations will also be able to see and study them.

Frank Preusser, director of research at the Getty Conservation Institute in Los Angeles, may have found a solution. He has designed a glass case filled with nitrogen instead of oxygen. Not only does the atmosphere in the case have very low humidity, but nitrogen is cheap and only has to be recharged every five or six years. A handwritten copy of Abraham Lincoln's Emancipation Proclamation is currently preserved this way.

Where Are They Now?

Mummies have ended up in some strange places. Napoleon sent mummies to the Louvre when he conquered Egypt in 1799. But in the damp climate of France, the mummies quickly deteriorated. They stank terribly and were buried in a hurry! Then, in 1830, France went through civil upheaval. Over 500 revolutionaries were killed and buried in a single spot—the same one where the rotting mummies had been buried! Ten years later, when officials dug up the revolutionary heroes' bodies to give them a proper burial ceremony, nobody could tell which bones were French and which were Egyptian. That's why today several hundred Frenchmen—and a few ancient

Egyptians—lie under the Bastille column in Paris.

In 1985 a woman in Memphis, Tennessee, cleaned out her attic. She took a gift from her great-uncle, who had been an explorer, to the local museum. It turned out to be one of the best-preserved mummy heads in existence.

In Illinois a private collector named Harlan J. Berk has been having trouble selling his 2,000-year-old mummy. The $50,000 price tag isn't the problem. The problem is a state law that says that any human remains transported outside the state must have a birth certificate—which Berk's mummy is definitely lacking!

In 1989 a mummy was found untouched in one of the most frequently looted places on earth—the Great Pyramid of Khufu. Not only that, but the mummy was 4,400 years old, making it the oldest Egyptian mummy ever found. And it is in amazingly good condition. The twenty-two-year-old, 4 foot 1 inch female is known as the "Smiling Mummy" because of the peaceful expression on her face.

Where is King Tutankhamen now? He is perhaps the only mummy at rest in his original tomb. But the objects he was buried with, considered some of the finest works of art in the world, are on display in Cairo's Egyptian Museum.

When King Tutankhamen's tomb was opened, many questions about ancient Egypt were answered. But the young pharaoh has remained silent about one final mystery: Studies of Tutankhamen's corpse show that he died of a cerebral hemmorhage—the bleeding caused by blows to the back of his head.

Did the eighteen-year-old pharaoh die naturally—or was he *murdered?* We may never know.

How To Find a Mummy

You may not be able to see a completely unwrapped mummy. Even wrapped mummies are rarely exhibited. Usually museums display only mummy cases and the objects that ancient Egyptians had buried with them.

Call your local museum to find out if they have any mummies on display. The most extensive Egyptian exhibits in the United States are in museums on the East Coast, but mummies can be seen in other museums throughout the country. The following museums have permanent Egyptian exhibits, or exhibits including mummies:

The Brooklyn Museum
200 Eastern Parkway
Brooklyn, New York 11231
(718) 638–5000

The Metropolitan Museum of Art
1000 Fifth Avenue
New York, New York 10028
(212) 535–7710 or (212) 879–5500

The Museum of Fine Arts in Boston
465 Huntington Avenue
Boston, Massachusetts 02115
(617) 267-9300

Natural History Museum
900 Exposition Boulevard
Los Angeles, California 90007
(213) 744-3414

Oriental Institute Museum
1155 East 58th Street
Chicago, Illinois 60637
(312) 702-9521